the Cabot Trail

STEEL TOWN PUBLISHING

Sydney, Nova Scotia

For Katheryn

Edited by Ron Keough

Designed by Jacqueline Ranahan

With thanks to
Les Amis du Plein Air
Parks Canada
David Lawley
Robert Boudreau
Ronald Caplan
Whale Cruisers Ltd.
Lionel Serroul

Photographs by
WARREN GORDON M.P.A

Text by
DAVID A. HARLEY

Published by: Steel Town Publishing
Gordon Photographic Ltd.
367 Charlotte Street, Sydney,
Nova Scotia Canada B1P 1C8

Gordon Warren, 1951 -

ISBN 0-929116-52-6

1. Cape Breton Island (N.S.)
Description of the Cabot Trail, travel
Views I.Title

Printed in China

INTRODUCTION

There is a soulfulness to Cape Breton Island that gladdens the heart. It is carried on the legacy of centuries of hard work, hard living and hard times, and of the determination and resolve that comes from such experiences. It manifests itself in the outpouring of Cape Breton culture — the music, the songs, the dancing, and the uncommon goodness and decency of Cape Bretoners.

Cape Breton's "soul" is also the island itself — the interplay of land and water; the dramatic contrasts between the seasons; the scenic beauty of highlands, lowlands, waterways, fields and, forests.

No where else is this soulfulness best exemplified than in the highlands, the rugged northern tip of the island. It is a landscape of boreal forests, tundra-like vegetation, glacial till, geological faults, and wilderness shoreline; a habitat for moose, eagles, lynx, salmon, and whales; a community of fishing villages, tourist towns, dairy farms, and fish plants. It is a place that captures the imagination, dazzles the senses and calms the nerves.

Through it all runs the Cabot Trail, a vital communications and transportation life-line, and also one of North America's most scenic drives. The undisputed gem of Maritime Canada, is a tourist attraction of international renown and fame.

For resident Cape Bretoners "doing the Trail" is an annual event. For Cape Bretoners living away, a visit home is not complete without an excursion around the Trail. For thousands of travellers around the world, a tour of the Cabot Trail becomes a memorable experience to be cherished forever.

Warren Gordon's photographs reveal the scenery, industry and people of this special corner of Atlantic Canada capturing the beauty and grandeur of Cape Breton's highland masterpiece.

Consider this book an armchair adventure of the Cabot Trail. May it bring back fond memories, or inspire you to create your own.

This text was written in memory of my father, Alex Harley, who first showed me the wonder and the beauty of the Cabot Trail.

David Harley

THE HISTORY OF THE CABOT TRAIL

Before the highway there was the sea… the road of commerce and communication. Adventurers, fishermen and merchant sailors explored the Nova Scotia coastline with skill and daring. They settled the coves and coastal plains and exploited the fishery and Maritime trading routes. In winter, when drift-ice prevented sea travel, villagers along the rim of Northern Cape Breton followed Mi'Kmaq trails along the coast or through the woods. It was not pleasant or efficient travel and by the end of the Great War communities in the northern reaches were petitioning for a permanent road around the highlands.

North America's passion for the automobile hastened the commissioning of the Cabot Trail. Already there was a decent road from Baddeck to Margaree Harbour, with a cart track from there to Cheticamp. On the north shore, a rough road followed the coast from St. Ann's Harbour to base of Cape Smokey. But for

those communities "north of Smokey" the sea remained the only highway.

Even in the early years the tourism potential of a highway around northern Cape Breton was recognized. In January 1924, the Victoria County Municipal Council urged the provincial government to construct a road from Cape North to Cheticamp claiming "this road would no doubt be the most popular drive in North America." A.S. MacMillian, Nova Scotia's Minister of Highways in the 1920's was a strong supporter of a paved road around the highlands. At the time the only pavement in the entire province was the ten-mile stretch from Halifax to Bedford along the shores of Bedford Basin. Work began in 1926. By the fall of 1927, the 24-mile section between Cheticamp and Pleasant Bay had been completed. In 1930 the Cape Breton Tourist Association noted that "beyond Pleasant Bay there is as yet nothing but a bridle path… but predicted, that once completed… " such a motor outing would have no peer in all the American realm."

On Oct. 15, 1932 Nova Scotia Premier Gordon S. Harrington set off the dynamite charge that removed the final rock barrier on North Mountain. Reverend R.L. MacDonald of Inverness was the first person to drive a car over the completed Cabot Trail. Still, it took 11 hours of slow, deliberate driving to go from Cheticamp to Dingwall.

The creation of Cape Breton Highlands National Park in 1936 hastened improvements to the roadway. From 1936 to 1940 the Cabot Trail was reconstructed. This phase included the elimination of the climb over French Mountain in favour of a new route along Jumping Brook.

In 1948, eleven miles between North Ingonish and Neil's Harbour were rebuilt to follow the Atlantic coastline. More construction was undertaken in 1951 with work on the sections from Ingonish to Effie's Brook and from North Mountain to Pleasant Bay. Guard rails were added in 1952 and paving was finally started in 1954 on the Atlantic side. The paving of the Cabot Trail was completed in 1961.

Today, the Cabot Trail is a safe, smooth, modern highway. Numerous pull-offs encourage travellers to take in the scenic views, interpretive sites, geology, flaura and fauna of the national park. It is a marvel of engineering skill and highway construction; a vital transportation link for the scattered coastal communities; and a thrilling scenic drive unparalleled in the Western hemisphere.

The Victoria County Court House in Baddeck marks the official start of the Cabot Trail, but most travelers make the turn at Exit 7, Trans-Canada 105, for their trip to the highlands.

The Red Barn Restaurant & Gift Shops makes a colorful start to one of North America's most scenic drives. Featuring an eclectic blend of recorded Maritime music, home-made quilts, mini putt golf, and a "Taste of Nova Scotia" restaurant, the Red Barn sets a festive mood for the coming adventure.

From Exit 7 in Nyanza, the Cabot Trail goes right for the highlands, making a 500-foot climb over Hunter's Mountain. This extensively logged area is an important source of softwood lumber for the Stora pulp and paper mill at Port Hawkesbury.
The mountain is criss-crossed by countless dirt roads and woodland trails that are used by hikers, hunters, and snowmobilers. The Nova Scotia Snowmobile Association holds its major winter safari through these mountainous back roads in mid-March.

At the base of Hunter's Mountain the landscape opens up to reveal the flat, wide swath of a highland glen. The valley of the Middle River has been productive farmland and woodlot since the first Scottish pioneers settled this area in 1812. On both sides of the river, hayfields and cattle barns dominate the landscape. Gairlock and Gilanders Mountains rise to the west; the Big Barrens loom from the north and the river flows through the middle of the green fields.

In the vicinity are three, 19th-century stone houses built by the Scottish pioneers. They remain as testimony to the resourcefulness and skills of those first settlers.

e Cabot Trail leaves the Middle River Valley, it passes the lakes district which is comprised of three small n lakes — First Lake O'Law, Second Lake O'Law, and Lake. At the provincial picnic park on the edge of

Second Lake O'Law the placid water of the pool reflects the greenery of the opposite shore — the hills known as The Three Sisters.

As the Cabot Trail enters the Margaree Valley, Egypt Road leads to The Normaway Inn, one of the oldest hostelries in the province. Built in 1928, the inn is known for fine dining and lively evening entertainment. Champion Cape Breton fiddlers and piano players polish off dozens of strathspeys, jigs, and reels well into the summer night as local aficionados introduce visitors to energetic and infectious square sets of Cape Breton-style country dances. The best dancers usually claim spots right in front of the stage, but there's always room for enthusiastic amateurs. Yahoo!

"There's nothing quite like it in the province," says Normaway owner David MacDonald. "Sometimes the tourists are overwhelmed...it can get quite exuberant. They are especially impressed with the high quality of musicianship...we showcase the best players in the land."

The communities along the Margaree River were established at the turn of the 19th century, first by pioneers from England and later by settlers from Ireland and Scotland. The so-called "French" side of the river is at East Margaree where Acadian pioneers established farms in the early 1800's.

Harrison Hill Bed and Breakfast, home of concert pianist Robin Harrison, stands on a small rise overlooking Margaree Forks. Robin often displays his musical virtuosity during impromptu evening recitals in his beloved studio to the surprise and delight of his guests. "When my wife Marilyn and I decided to open our bed and breakfast and "retire," neither of us imagined how busy and involved we would become in the artistic life of our community and Cape Breton as a whole. We both particularly love working with the super young people of the island."

The Coady and Tompkins Library is named for local activists Moses Coady and Jimmy Tompkins. The two first cousins used their standing as Roman Catholic priests to advance the cause of social justice and economic independence for the working class by helping to establish the cooperative movement.

Canadian novelist and Cape Breton native Hugh MacLennan once called the Margaree River, "the nobelist stream in all of Nova Scotia."

The Margaree, which is made up of three rivers — the Northeast, Southwest and Margaree — has been an internationally-acclaimed salmon stream for more than a century. The late summer and fall salmon run still attracts anglers from around the world, many who come as much for the peaceful ambiance of the river and valley as they do for the sport.

The history of angling on the river is a compelling one, told with broad strokes and delicate care at the Margaree Salmon Museum. Housed in a former one-room schoolhouse, the museum has a fine collection of fishing tackle, poaching equipment, photographs of award-winning fish, maps, and scale-model reproductions of the river and its tributaries. The fishery is open from June to October. The biggest salmon caught on the Margaree was a 52.5-pound trophy taken in 1927 using a No. 6 Black Dose fly. In recent times an average of 2,000 fish annually are taken by rod and reel on the Margaree.

In this corner of Inverness County you still make hay while the sun shines. The large and lush hayfields that sweep down from the road to the water's edge like great, green blankets, produce some 6,000 acres of hay annually that is used to feed the some 500 head of cattle that pasture in the Margaree Valley. The hay is cut while moist and packaged in white, plastic wrapping. This allows it to ferment, preserving the nutrients. Valley farmers rely on this summer bounty to maintain their livestock throughout the winter.

Also grown and harvested here in Cape Breton's "breadbasket" is wheat, oats, and barley. In recent years the production of maple syrup by area residents has increased.

Margaree Harbour — The beach! The sunset! The lobster! There's no finer place on a summer's eve if you've got all three.

Here the river unobtrusively slides under the bridge and enters Northumberland Strait. To the left of the bridge is Margaree Harbour Beach one of the best swimming beaches on the Cabot Trail. The water is warm, there's plenty of sand, and the shore slopes gradually into the sun-dappled waves.

Across the bridge, a left turn leads to the small craft harbour where a large fishing fleet brings home lobster and snow crab in summer. There's a small picnic area near the breakwater and a seafood "shack" that sells live and cooked lobster, crab and clams.

Margaree Harbour is where you'll find "The Boat That Wouldn't Float," the subject of a humorous book by Canadian author Farley Mowatt. The boat is part of Schooner Village Gift Shop, operated by Connecticut native John May who came to Cape Breton for the climate: "Not too humid in summer; not much snow in winter." "I also came for the piping which is some of the best in the Celtic realm."

At Cap Lemoine is one of the Cabot Trail's unique attractions — Joe's Scarecrow Gallery. This rag-tag collection of handmade, wooden scarecrows was the brainchild of the late Joe Delaney. His garden and the handful of colourful scarecrows he created caught the attention of passing motorists who stopped to take photographs and chat with Joe. Soon the garden was abandoned and the scarecrows, including the likenesses of George Bush and Margaret Thatcher, were moved closer to the road, creating an instant attraction. Sometimes celebrities and world leaders such as Cape Breton's own **General John Cabot Trail,** the comic creation of author Dave Harley, drop in to admire the eye-catching display.

"Yes, bys, when me and Mrs. Trail do the Trail we always come to Joe's Scarecrows to inspect the troops and salute the tourists. No crows at Joe's… no flies on me."

Joe's has free parking, free admission and a decidedly cheeky attitude. Is there one that looks like you?

Lime-green shingles, houses attached to barns, a horse's head carved into a fencepost, and the tri-coloured Acadian are all signs that you've reached the Acadian Shore of the Cabot Trail. From Belle Cote to Belle March the language, food, crafts, and customs take on a decidedly Gallic flair. Architecture by design or whimsey — who's to know? The snappy colours? — could be leftover boat paint, or a need for self expression. Visit the local craft shops and galleries for the true artistes. C'est tres bien!

The landscape is different, too — a flat, mostly treeless coastal plain with a rough, serrated shoreline battered by wind and ice from the Gulf of St. Lawrence. On stormy days the high winds bring great waves of crashing surf to the shore, some of it landing as plumes of foam on the highway of the Cabot Trail.

From folk-art to French-flavoured food and speech, the fishing village of Cheticamp is the main repository of the Acadian culture on Cape Breton Island. The wonderful craft shops, fine restaurants, deep-sea fishing charters, and whale-watching tours make Cheticamp more than just an overnight stop.

The economic impact of the Cabot Trail on northern communities is best illustrated in Cheticamp. In 1956, the town had a population of 1,036. Some thirty years later, Cheticamp's population has tripled and the community has become a popular destination for visitors.

The Cabot Trail is Cheticamp's main street and it passes by its best-known landmark — St. Peter's Church. This massive stone edifice was built in 1892 using stone from Cheticamp Island. The heavy material was brought over the harbour ice by horse and sleigh.

Youth choir director Michel Aucoin, encourages impressive performances from his talented young choral group, "L'echo des Montagnes". Michel believes that it was Cheticamp's isolation in the last century that preserved its culture: "Now it is pure and untainted… we can export the real thing… true Acadian culture through our music, language, crafts and other artistic expressions."

At the other end of the village stands the Doryman, a traditional Cape Breton tavern and also a Cheticamp cultural hot-spot. On Saturday afternoon the beer parlour comes alive with a genuine Acadian "Gros tyme" with fiddles, guitars, and sometimes a spoons player to keep time to the Acadian/Scottish-style repertoire.

GROCERY
H EPICERIE

CO-OP

REPAS MEALS
ACADIEN

MUSEUM &
HANDCRAFTS

Cheticamp has long been known for the quality of its crafts and folk-art. The women of the village were especially skilled in the needle-arts — knitting, crocheting, and rug-hooking — so much so that a multimillion dollar cottage industry has developed.

Les Trois Pignons on Main Street, is the headquarters for La Societe St. Pierre, which promotes Acadian culture, heritage and genealogy. It is the home of the Dr. Elizabeth LeFort Gallery and Museum.

Elizabeth LeFort is Cheticamp's best-known "artist in wool" and her hand-hooked tapestries hang in the White House, The Vatican and Buckingham Palace.

Cheticamp wood carver William Roach is an accomplished folk artist whose work is displayed all across North America. His cottage-size gallery, at the north end of town, is chock-a-bloc with a menagerie of weird-looking birds and animals. His brightly painted gulls, eagles, and woodpeckers peek from every corner of his shop and wood shed.

"The Cabot Trail is good for business… but not so good for the artist," says Roach "In summer I'm too busy with visitors to devote time to carving."

David Lawley, author of **"A Natural History Guide to the Cabot Trail"** and a naturalist with Parks Canada says: "The Cape Breton highlands are rich in flora and fauna and the park makes things fairly accessible. Take the park trails, and walk the shorelines. Wildlife viewing here can be very satisfying for both the novice and the experienced observer."

Where To See The Wildlife:

Moose — Benjie's Lake, top of McKenzie Mountain; top of North Mountain, dawn or dusk.

Bald Eagles — Shoreline, St. Ann's Harbour between North River Bridge and Gaelic College. Try St. Ann's picnic park.

Whales — Whale-watching tours from Cheticamp, Pleasant Bay, Dingwall, Ingonish Ferry. Pilot whales sometimes are seen in Pleasant Bay from look-offs on McKenzie Mountain.

Common Terns — Summer nesting colony atop the rock pinnacle at the end of Middle Head hiking trail, behind Keltic Lodge, Ingonish Beach.

Canada Geese — Shoreline shallows at end of Baddeck Bay, route 205.

Sora Rail — Marsh, North Beach Picnic Park, dusk, Ingonish Beach

Red Fox, White-tailed deer — Highlands Golf Links, Ingonish Beach, dusk.

At the park's visitor centre, maps, and brochures are available. An exhibit of the park's wildlife is on display. The centre also houses a nature bookstore, the largest in the region, with a great collection of field guides, photo books, history books, tapes, and souvenirs.

COYOTE

LYNX
LYNX DU CANADA

Along the Cabot Trail there are 18 federal Small Craft Harbours where boats are moored, the catch is landed, repairs are made and the eternal vagaries of the weather and fishing grounds are pondered with parliamentary-like wisdom.

Tourists are welcome. It's a chance to see an industry that is part of the heritage and culture of Maritime Canada; maybe an opportunity to buy fresh lobster right from the boat. Park away from the shore. Watch your step.

Cape Breton Highlands National Park begins just past Cheticamp. The 360-square-mile refuge protects the largest and most rugged wilderness area in Maritime Canada. Here the Cabot Trail weaves its way between the steep slopes of the Grand Falaise and French Mountain, and the craggy cliffs of Cap Rouge.

Fifteenth-century explorer John Cabot first extolled the riches of the North Atlantic fishery. The fishery is the economic mainstay of northern Cape Breton. Lobster, crab and ground fish are the principal catch.

The way to experience the northern Cape Breton coastline is by boat. There are deep-sea fishing charters out of Cheticamp, Pleasant Bay and Ingonish, as well as numerous whale-watching tours that follow the pods of pilot whales, revealing sea caves, waterfalls, shipwrecks, seabird colonies, and more.

Some adventurers explore the coast by kayak which provides an even more intimate look at this remote corner of Atlantic Canada.

Great walls of wave-battered cliffs rise hundreds of feet from sea level all along the northern tip of Cape Breton Island. This is the haunt of whales and cormorants, seals and eagles, black bear, and moose.

The National Park maintains several hiking trails along the coastline that allow you to explore the rocky beaches and coastal woods.

There is a magnificent wilderness seacoast campground at Fishing Cove at the base of MacKenzie Mountain, where a small community existed at the turn of the century. The campground is reached after a rugged 6-mile-long hike along the Fishing Cove River to the coast.

The view from the French Mountain look-off, showcasing the steep cliffs that cascade to meet the broad, blue Gulf of St. Lawrence, is one of the most recognizable images of Canada's landscape.

Along the shore here are the remains of an Acadian fishing community — Cap Rouge. At the turn of the century about 30 families lived in the lee of the mountain sustaining themselves through the lucrative cod fishery. All that remains today is the foundation of the wharf.

In the early days of the Trail, this section of the highway was one of the most treacherous as it made a tortuous direct climb over French Mountain. So narrow was the roadway that motorists were obliged to start their journey early in the morning for fear of meeting a car coming from the other direction. Five to seven miles per hour was the normal driving speed. In the 1940's the route was changed to follow the valley of Jumping Brook making for a less-precipitous ascent and a far more scenic view.

For an even more dramatic perspective of this scene, hikers can walk the Skyline Trail which goes right to the edge of the cliff on the far side of the gorge. Wave to the cars on the Trail and they'll wonder: "How did they get way out there?"

In late May runners participating in the annual Cabot Trail 24-Hour Relay Race stream down French Mountain in the dark of night, the green beams from their glow-stick batons bouncing eerily off the ocean mist. This race is one of the most popular relays in North America, attracting some 50 teams of 17 runners from Canada and the United States.

At the top of French Mountain, the Cabot Trail reaches an elevation of 1,492 feet. Here the stunted spruce and boggy lakes dominate the landscape of this wild and windswept plateau.

"Psst - wanna see some moose tracks? How about a carnivorous plant?" The secrets of the highland heights are revealed at the Bog Walk, where insect-eating Pitcher Plants are easily spotted from the boardwalk. And yes, those hoof marks in the mud are made by moose!

This section of the Cabot Trail takes winter at its worst. Raging blizzards and hurricane-force winds can easily strand the most fearless of drivers. Emergency shelters are strategically placed near the road to aid in rescue.

The snowplough crews who maintain the highland highways in winter are the jet pilots of northern Cape Breton and their work is regarded with heroic admiration. It's every grade school student's dream to drive the plow that clears the Cabot Trail.

The village of Pleasant Bay was settled in the early 1820's by Scottish pioneers who made a subsistence living by farming and fishing. Theirs was a life of hardship and isolation. In winter, massive ice flows prevented travel by boat. The only route to Cheticamp was by foot path over the mountains. Still, they say, the mailman made the journey once a week, although letters were scarce between the Gaelic-speaking Scots and the Acadian French of Cheticamp.

On MacKenzie Mountain an interpretive display tells the story of the MacKenzie River valley forest fire of 1947. The fire raged unchecked for 12 days, fuelled by strong winds and tinder-dry spruce. The villagers were rescued by sea during a daring nighttime evacuation by the Cheticamp fishing fleet.

Today, Pleasant Bay is a prosperous coastal community with a busy small craft harbour.

Leaving Pleasant Bay the Cabot Trail re-enters the National Park through the Grand Anse river valley, an area of great natural beauty.

"From the lone shieling of the misty island
Mountains divide us and the waste of seas —
Yet still the blood is strong, the heart is highland
And we in dreams behold the Hebrides."
— Oxford Book of English Verse, 1829, attributed to John Galt

This verse is inscribed on a plaque at the Lone Shieling, a replica of a Scottish crofter's hut built by the National Park Service at the behest of Donald MacIntosh. A Pleasant Bay native, he willed more than 1,000 acres of the Grand Anse river valley to the crown in 1934.

This small park contains the last remaining virgin hardwood forest on the eastern seaboard of North America. Here some of the trees grow as high as 120 feet. The sugar maples, beech, oak, birch, and red maples are estimated to be about 350 years old. This is a rare and special place, the northern and eastern limit of the Acadian forest. The moist slopes of the river gorge house a treasure-trove of rare, arctic-alpine plants — at least 27 different kinds. The valley floor abounds in an array of some two dozen different species of ferns.

There are rare animals here, too, such as the rock vole, found nowhere else in Nova Scotia, and the Gaspe shrew, whose only other habitat is the Gaspe Peninsula of Quebec.

The Cabot Trail climbs 1,460 feet to the top of North Mountain, which is part of a massive geological fault. The Aspy Fault runs more than 18 miles from the ocean at Bay St. Lawrence inland to Big Intervale.

The descent of North Mountain includes wonderful views of North Aspy River valley and South Mountain, as well as glimpses of Beulach Ban Falls, a narrow splash of white amid the hillside greenery. The falls are reached from the Cabot Trail via a dirt road to the right of the warden's house at the base of the mountain.

From the parking lot at the falls, is a mountain hiking trail that pushes deep into the heart of an amazingly thick hardwood forest. At the end of the climb, at the top of South Mountain, the forest changes to the boreal realm of the highland plateau. The richness and purity of the wilderness experience is easily found within the Cape Breton Highlands Park

The Cabot Trail exits the national park at Big Interval and enters the Sunrise Valley where it passes through the farm of Kenneth MacKinnon. MacKinnon's farm house was built in 1879 and the barn, which sits on the edge of the trail, dates from 1929. MacKinnon sells maple syrup and rhubarb from a makeshift market in his woodshed and admits that living on the world-famous Cabot Trail has its pluses and minuses. "Most times I love it here, but it's not so famous in February when you are stuck on North Mountain waiting for the snowplow."

In June of 1497, John Cabot, a native of Genoa, Italy, under auspices of the waterfront merchants of Bristol, England and flying the English flag, anchored his ship "Matthew" on the beach near Cape North. Cape Breton was discovered and British presence was established in North America. As the story goes, John Cabot did the front-nine at The Highlands Links, played bingo at St. Peter's hall, had lunch at Keltic Lodge then went on to discover Newfoundland!

Each June the Cape Breton Historical Society re-enacts John Cabot's arrival at Cabot Landing Provincial Park, maintaining the legend of Cabot's exploration of the New World and discovery of Cape Breton Island.

The long sandy beach at Cabot Landing is one of several strands of sand found along this shore. Some are barrier beaches that protect shallow salt-water lagoons; others lie exposed to the sea and the daily freshness of the open ocean; others are tiny shingles of sand and rocks sequestered in the corners of hidden coves. All are worthy of the time and effort it takes to explore them.

On August 16, 1858, the first-trans-Atlantic Morse Code message from Europe to North America was sent via underwater cable. The 2,500-mile-long cable came ashore at Aspy Bay to a crude hut at the bottom of Cape North.

Cape North was settled by pioneers from Scotland in the early 1800's. Gaelic was the language of home and field. Residents did not learn English unless they attended school.

This is the most northerly point on the Cabot Trail, but you can go further north by taking a side trip to visit the coastal communities of Bay St. Lawrence, Capstick, Dingall and Meat Cove.

On the road to Bay St. Lawrence is Cabot Landing Provincial Park, where a monument to explorer John Cabot looks out over the barrier beach and lagoon.

The northern reaches of Nova Scotia attract an uncommon breed of people. Some come for the isolation, for the wilderness challenge; others come to escape the clang and bustle of city life.

Fred, a fisherman from Maine who has strong Nova Scotia ties, arrived in Bay St. Lawrence with Margrit from Switzerland. They came for the sea, to make a home and built their own boat. And when it was finished, they got married on it! Their self-built ketch, "The Double Crow", is a replica of "The Spray", the boat made famous by Nova Scotian navigator Joshua Slocum, who, in 1897, became the first person to singlehandedly sail around the world.

From Cape North the Cabot Trail re-enters the National Park at Effie's Brook and takes a direct, inland route to Neil's Harbour. Many travellers have discovered the Alternate Scenic Route which follows the coast past the villages of Smelt Brook, White Point, and New Haven. This route climbs over small headlands and dips into tiny coves where brightly painted Cape Islanders take shelter from the Atlantic swells.

Neil's Harbour borders a picturesque cove which features a breakwater, public wharf, lighthouse, and chowder house overlooking the Atlantic. In mid-August the village celebrates its seafaring heritage with its Linger-By-The-Sea-Festival.

The Atlantic side of the Cabot Trail has a softer edge to its beauty than that of the Gulf coast. Here the mountains slope gently to the shore and there are many coves, points, headlands, and sandy beaches. One of the best beaches is at Black Brook where the national park maintains a picnic site and nearby campground.

From the parking lot of the picnic area there's a short hiking trail to the open ocean at Squeaker's Hole, a v-shaped slice of shoreline carved into the granite rocks.

North Ingonish is the home of landscape artist Christopher Gorey, a Massachusetts native who has painted images of this coast since his arrival in 1974.

"It's not something I think about on a day-to-day basis, but when I return from my travels and see this natural beauty I realize this is spectacular…this is my inspiration."

A well-travelled road leads from the Cabot Trail to Mary Ann Falls, the most popular waterfall in the highlands with its steady burst of white water churning through a rocky gorge.

The unpaved road to Mary Ann Falls was part of the original Cabot Trail, but the highway was rebuilt in the 1940's to follow a more scenic route along the seashore.

From Broad Cove the Trail continues to skirt the coastline revealing cobblestone beaches and granite points. There are pull-offs at Broad Cove, McKinnon's Cove, Green Cove, and Lackie's Head. Green Cove has a self-guiding interpretive trail that describes some of the vegetation that clings to life along this delicate margin of land.

In May and June the Ingonish lobster boats work close to shore. So close, in fact, you can perch on a shoreline boulder and watch the Cape Islanders putter from buoy to buoy, hauling the treasured traps with their tasty cargo. That three-pounder might just be your supper tonight if you dine at one of the local seafood restaurants.

The Ingonish area is made up of five connecting villages — North Ingonish, Ingonish Centre, Ingonish Beach, Ingonish Harbour, and Ingonish Ferry — and is the commercial centre for the Atlantic side of the Cabot Trail.

The Ingonish area was first visited by Portuguese fishermen as early as 1521. It is believed that they gave the name "Ingonish" to the area. There is, however, evidence that early man was present here. In 1975 a team of archeologists uncovered a cache of pre-historic bones on Ingonish Island that are believed to be 7,000 years old. There is also evidence of prehistoric settlement at Clyburn Brook. The Scots and English took up permanent settlement here in the early part of the 19th century. Schools and churches were built in the 1850's as the coastal communities took root, relying mainly on the fishery for economic stability.

The Ingonish area became a noted resort community even before the completion of the Cabot Trail. Well-to-do visitors often came by boat, including, Henry Clay Corson, an Ohio industrialist. He was so entranced with the view that he built his summer mansion atop Middle Head peninsula in the 1930's. Today, Corson's summer retreat is known as The Keltic Lodge, and has been operated as a resort since 1947. Mr Corson's wife was the last resident of the lodge and it is said that her ghost sometimes appears near the stone fireplace just before the evening meal. If you see her, invite her in for tea!

Middle Head overlooks Ingonish Beach, one of the most popular seaside destinations in all of Cape Breton. The ocean water is cool and bracing, so many sunbathers do a double dip — the ocean first, then the warmer waters of the sheltered Freshwater Lake located just beyond the dunes. The beach park also has playing fields, lifeguard service, picnic area, and tennis courts.

The jewel of the Ingonish area is the Highlands Links Golf Course. This Stanley Thompson-designed layout is regarded as one of the finest golfing venues in all of North America. The course begins at the base of the Middle Head Peninsula and follows the Clyburn Brook into the Highlands.

The development of Ski Cape Smokey in the early 1970's made Ingonish both a winter as well as a summer resort destination. The 1,000-foot ski hill has the longest vertical run in Maritime Canada. In 1987, Ingonish hosted both the downhill and cross-country skiing competitions of the Canada Winter Games.

For many years the imposing climb over Cape Smokey kept the Ingonish area isolated from the rest of the world. It was the weekly visits from the coastal steamers from Sydney and North Sydney that brought food, tools, supplies, mail, and people to and from the villages "north of Smokey." For some 50 years these coastal supply boats — all named "Aspy" — maintained a vital link between northern Cape Breton and the world beyond.

In 1968, the side of the Cape Smokey was burned badly by a forest fire claiming some four thousand acres, destroying four homes and several barns and forcing the evacuation of about 40 residents. Regeneration has been slow, but there are now shrubs, small trees and grasses where once only burned tree trunks and barren round appeared.

Today the drive over Smokey is one of the most thrilling along the Cabot Trail. At the top is a picnic park with spectacular views of the coastline. In spite of the impressive view, Cape Smokey is the smallest of the major mountains along the Trail reaching some 850 feet above sea level.

It is estimated that some half-a-million motor vehicles travel the Cabot Trail annually. Since its paving in 1962 the trail has become popular with cyclists. About 4,000 cyclists each summer meet the challenge of this once-in-a-lifetime ride. Besides the main highway there are many side roads that are suitable for cycling.

Here is a collection of alternative rides.

Middle River Valley This roadway is located on the west side of the Middle River. Exit the Cabot Trail at Upper Middle River at the base of Hunter's Mountain. Cross the bridge at the cemetery and go in either direction. To the left the road goes all the way to the Trans-Canada Highway over a steep climb; a right turn goes over hilly terrain and returns to the Cabot Trail about 5 miles later. This route gets less traffic than the main road through Middle River.

The Margaree Valley: Take the Egypt Road off the Cabot Trail and cycle the side roads of the river valley. The best pavement and flattest roads are found in Northeast Margaree and Margaree Centre.

Plateau This is the Cheticamp "back road" and is a good way to avoid the traffic of Cheticamp's main street and still get to the national park. The road goes from the Cabot Trail at Point Cross to Belle Marche and returns to the Trail at Petit Etang just before the park entrance. There are several cross roads from Belle Marche into the village. The road climbs steadily up the side of the mountain — a tough climb, but with wonderful views of Cheticamp Island and Cheticamp Harbour.

Route 312: This is the road that takes you to the Englishtown ferry. It's a very flat road from the Cabot Trail turn off at Barrachois River all the way to the ferry dock. The road goes along the scenic Jersey Cove sandbar which is a good spot for bird-watching. Avoid this highway Sunday evenings and holiday weekends.

Big Harbour This diversion goes from the Trans-Canada Highway near South Haven to the old ferry dock on the Bras d'Or Lake. It's about 12 miles, round-trip. There's one steep hill, but the rest of the road is fairly level. It skirts the north shore of Big Harbour which is a favourite fishing spot for bald eagles.

Baddeck River Valley This loop of about 13 miles begins and ends at Exit 9 of the Trans-Canada Highway north of the village of Baddeck and goes to Forks Baddeck along the Baddeck River. The road is hilly in part with little traffic.

From the base of Cape Smokey at the Barrachois River, the Cabot Trail stretches along a coastal plain. On this thin strip of and between the water and the mountain a handful of sparsely-settled villages hug the rocky shore.

This is Cape Breton's "North Shore," a coast that includes Wreck Cove, Breton Cove, and the western side of St. Ann's Bay. Small brooks and rivers cascade from the mountains helping to form barrachois ponds near the shore.

From the Barrachois River an interesting diversion follows Route 312 through River Bennett to the sandbar at Jersey Cove.

The sandbar is a great place for bird-watching and beach combing. Driftwood washes up on the exposed Atlantic side, while the sheltered harbour side of the bar attracts a variety of birds including gulls, cormorants, sandpipers, terns, ducks, and bald eagles.

At Indian Brook, the Cabot Trail turns right to follow the Barrachois River. This section is referred to as the St. Ann's Loop. The Trail winds through a highland glen, around the mouth of North River and along the south side of St. Ann's Harbour.

Indian Brook and the St. Ann's Loop boasts an unusually high concentration of crafts' people and artisans. Unique creations in wood, clay, porcelain, iron, fabric, rope, and leather can be found. Paintings, photographs, clothes, musical instruments and pottery can be purchased.

St. Ann's Harbour is 8 miles wide and 12 miles long and is bracketed by two giant hills — Murray Mountain which over-looks the mouth of North River and Kelly's Mountain which hangs over the entire eastern shoreline. St. Ann's Harbour, at one time, was a noted shipbuilding centre.

The small coves and marshes along the shore provide cover for a great variety of bird life. Kingfishers, mergansers, ducks, terns, Canada geese, and bald eagles are common. This is perhaps the best place along the Cabot Trail to spot bald eagles.

" And lovely girls
In pink ado
With costumes swell
Enrich the view"
— James P. Gillis, St.Ann's.

A highlight of any tour of the Cabot Trail is a visit to the Nova Scotia Gaelic College of Celtic Arts and Crafts. This is where Scottish tradition, "Cape Breton-style," lives and grows.

The institution offers a six-week summer session in a dozen different disciplines including Gaelic language, piping, drumming, Highland dancing, Scottish country dance, step-dancing, fiddle, and Celtic harp.

Executive Director of the college, Sam McPhee says the growth in popularity of the college since its beginning in a log cabin in 1937 speaks for itself: "We instruct 500 students. They come to us from across North America and from around the world. Our standards are well-respected internationally."

The Gaelic College Pipe and Drum band is one of the best in the world, an award-winning ensemble that plays with great skill and style. A chance to hear them play and see them march in full regalia should not be missed.

The culmination of summer studies is the annual Gaelic Mod, a week-long Celtic celebration with music, dancing, and piping competitions as well as evening entertainment. In August, the College hosts the St. Ann's Highland Gathering featuring the traditional Scottish heavyweight events such as the hammer toss and stone throw.

From St. Ann's Harbour the Cabot Trail proceeds west along the Trans-Canada Highway toward Baddeck. Along this section the charming place-names of South Haven and Glen Tosh speak of Scottish pioneers.

The hillside scenery is especially appealing in the fall when the hardwood trees put on their dazzling display of colour.

The village of Baddeck is the commercial centre for the southern end of the Cabot Trail and is one of Canada's great summer resort communities. This picturesque anchorage is home to 800 residents and offers first-rate accommodations, fine dining, and fascinating gift shops. The village fairly bursts with activity from May to October as tourists come to begin (or end) their Cabot Trail journey, and boaters from around the world come to sail the fog-free waters of the Bras d'Or Lake.

The village is the boating capital of Cape Breton. There are several charter boat tours available to take adventurers for excursions down the bay, around Red Head, over to Washabuck Point and past Spectacle Island, a wildlife sanctuary where Double-Crested Cormorants nest.

A boat tour of the Bras d'Or may include a sighting of the "Elsie", the 54-foot, two-masted yawl that was a wedding present from Dr. Alexander Graham Bell to his daughter Elsie and her husband Gilbert Grosvenor in 1917. Restored and refurbished by the owners of the prestigious Innverary Inn and Dundee Resort, the "Elsie's" clean lines and smart trim bring approving glances from knowledgeable sailors.

Across from Baddeck Bay, atop the Red Head peninsula, stands Beinn Breagh. This turn-of-the-century mansion was, for 35 years, the summer residence of Dr. Alexander Graham Bell inventor of the telephone. On the spectacular grounds of his retreat, Bell and his colleagues charged through a lifetime of daring adventures and ground-breaking scientific experiments

On February 21, 1909, Bell's Aerial Experimentation Association made history, when Baddeck native J.A.D. McCurdy took the Silver Dart for a 90-second jaunt over the ice of Baddeck Bay. This was the first powered flight in the British Empire. The next day's flight, without onlookers or press, was even more impressive — 40 minutes in the air including several turns around Red Head.

In 1919, Bells' team powered up the engines of the HD-4, a cigar-shaped hydrofoil that roared across the Bay at an incredible 70-miles-per-hour, a world record that stood for ten years. The stories of these achievements, as well as other experiments, are carefully and lovingly chronicled at the Baddeck museum that honours Dr. Bell — the Alexander Graham Bell National Historic Site, one of Canada's most popular museums.

Besides Dr. Bell, some other Baddeck luminaries include physician C. LaMont MacMillain who published his remembrances of life as a rural doctor in his book _Memories of A Cape Breton Doctor_.

Cape Breton-born novelist Hugh MacLennan, wrote about his 1939 tour of the Cabot Trail: "We made it at the cost of a blown tire, a nosebleed from the dust, a few dents in the chassis, a damaged spring, a cramp in my back and sore shoulders from working the steering wheel." MacLennan's chagrin would not ring true today. The Cabot Trail is a modern, well-maintained highway, comfortably explored in less than a day.

Yet, in spite of its growing popularity, it is still possible to make your own discoveries along the Cabot Trail — to set your own pace, to create your own adventures, and to discover new wonders on this unforgettable scenic highway.

"I have travelled around the world. I have seen the Canadian and American Rockies, the Andes, the Alps, and the Highlands of Scotland, but for simple beauty, Cape Breton outrivals them all."

Alexander Graham Bell

LIST OF PLATES

Cover… Ingonish
1. Cap Rouge
2. St. Ann's Bay
3. Presq'ile
4. Presq'ile
5. Cap Rouge
6. Map provided by the Nova Scotia Geometric Centre
7. The main street of Cheticamp in 1935 (LL)
   Cap Rouge, north of Cheticamp in 1933 (UR)
8. A typical section of the old Cabot Trail near North Mountain (UL)
   Cape Smokey (LL)
9. The Western coastline at Cap Rouge in 1934
10. Cap Rouge present day
11. Nyanza (UR)
    The Red Barn (Below)
12. Aucoin Farm, Middle River
13. Middle River
14. Middle River
15. Lake O'Law
16. Lake O'Law (UL)
    Egypt Road (Below)
17. Normaway Inn, Margaree Valley
    Fiddler by Gerard Deveau
18. Robin Harrison, Margaree Forks
19. Margaree Forks
20. Tompkins Pool, Margaree River
21. Margaree Salmon Museum
22. Margaree River
23. Margaree
24. John May (Left)
    Margaree Harbour (LR)

25. Margaree Harbour
26. Cap Lemoine (Left)
    Joe's Scarecrow Gallery (LR)
27. St. Joseph du Moine
28. St. Joseph du Moine
29. Grand Étang
30. "L'echo des Montagnes"
    St. Peter's Church, Cheticamp
31. Cheticamp
    Doryman Beverage Room (Inset)
32. Les Trois Pignons
    Elizabeth Lefort Tapestry Gallery (Inset)
33. William Roach, Cheticamp
34. Cormarants, Cap Rouge
35. David Lawley, Nature Interpretive Center, Cheticamp
36. Presq'ile Beach
37. Presq'ile
38/39 Cheticamp Island Lighthouse
40/41 Whale Cruisers, off Cap Rouge
42. Le Bloc Beach
43. Robert Boudreau, Cap Rouge
44. Cap Rouge
45. Jumping Cove Brook Valley
46. Fishing Cover River
47. MacKenzie Mountain
48/49 Pleasant Bay
50. Lone Shieling, Grand Anse Valley
51. Grand Anse Valley
52. Kenneth MacKinnon, Sunrise Valley
53. The Tom Saylor, Aspy Bay
    Daryl MacLean entertains her family, the Markland Resort, Dingwall (Inset)
54. John Cabot Monument, Aspy Bay
55. Aspy Bay
56. Bay St. Lawrence

57. Bay St. Lawrence
58. Neil's Harbour
59. Neil's Harbour
60. Black Brook Beach (LL)
    Chris Gorey, Ingonish (UR)
61. King's Point, North Bay, Ingonish
62. Mary Ann Falls
63. Warren Brook
64. The Keltic Lodge (UL)
    Ingonish Beach (LL)
65. The Highlands Links, Ingonish
66. Ski Cape Smokey, Ingonish
67. Cape Smokey
68. Smokey Mountain
70. North Shore
71. Morrison Farm, Wreck Cove
72. River Bennet
73. Barrachois River
74. Claire Ryder, Tarbot
75. John C. Roberts, Greg Mason, Indian Brook
76. Barrachois River, Tarbot Vale (UL)
    North River (LL)
77. St. Anns Bay
78/79 The Gaelic College, St. Ann's Bay
80. Glenvalley United Church, South Haven
81. South Haven
82. Baddeck
83. The Amoeba (UR)
    Regatta Week, Baddeck (LR)
84. The Elsie, Baddeck
85. Beinn Breagh   Alexander Graham Bell Museum, Baddeck.   (Inset)
86. Cap Rouge
Back Cover… Northwestern Cabot Trail

WARREN GORDON
Master of Photographic Arts

Since 1973, Warren Gordon has operated Gordon Photographic Limited, a major photographic studio and scenic gallery in downtown Sydney. He is recognized internationally for his portrait, group, industrial, aerial and landscape work. Although he is most closely associated with his Cape Breton Island canvas, Mr. Gordon has photographed the rest of Canada, as well as Asia, Europe, the Caribbean and the Rocky Mountains. Today, Mr. Gordon operates a fully digital studio with his wife, Katheryn, who shares his passion for capturing the world through the digital eye. Katheryn Gordon brings her own creative touch to her work. An accomplished oil painter, Katheryn combines portraiture and paintings in a medium she calls *digital fantasies.*

Mr. Gordon has published ten books of Cape Breton photographs:

Images of Cape Breton	*Island of Ghosts*
Cape Breton, Island of Islands	*Cape Breton Pictorial Cookbook*
Cape Breton Address Book	*The Cabot Trail*
Cape Breton, A Place Apart	*Cape Breton Island*
Jewel of the Atlantic: The Nova Scotia Story	*Baddeck: Heart of Cape Breton*
Cape Breton Portfolio	

DAVID A. HARLEY, BA

A native Cape Bretoner, David is a busy Maritime performer and writer with a variety of credits to his resume. He is best known as the creator of General John Cabot Trail, a comic character who has appeared on radio, television and stage for the past fifteen years. Mr. Harley has also written two hit songs: *Workin At The Woolco (Manager Trainee Blues)*, and *Let's Go Santa*, as well as two tapes of comedy material as General John Cabot Trail. His performance credits include an appearance in the original Rise and Follies, guest appearances on Royal Canadian Air Farce and Madly Off In All Directions. For some 15 Years he wrote travel articles for the Nova Scotia Department of Tourism and now through his publishing company - Tour-Lit = writes freelance travel articles for newspapers and magazines. Dave Harley has travelled extensively throughout Maritime Canada, but considers Cape Breton Island his favorite destination. The Cabot Trail is his first book.

PHOTO BY KRISTY READ

Visit **gordonphoto.com** for more information on the art of Warren and Katheryn Gordon

 Professional Photographers of Canada

Published by

GORDON PHOTOGRAPHIC LTD
Steeltown Publishing, 367 Charlotte Street,
Sydney, Nova Scotia, B1P 1E1
902.564.5665, gordonphoto@ns.sympatico.ca
www.gordonphoto.com

Order your copy of **CAPE BRETON ISLAND**
Price $29.95 Cdn. add 6% GST
Mailing in Canada, add $4.00
Mailing in USA, add $6.00

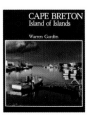